Military Strategy:
Thoughts Toward a Critique

Military Strategy

Thoughts toward a critique

Walter Jajko

The Institute of World Politics Press

The Institute of World Politics Press, Washington 20036
© 2014 by Walter Jajko
All rights reserved. Published 2014
First edition

ISBN-13: 978-0615979113
ISBN-10: 0615979114

Military Strategy:
Thoughts Toward a Critique

For many citizens, military strategy seems to be either obviously simple or simply incomprehensible. For most, it is arcane, esoteric, and, in its exercise, seemingly ill-used, poorly practiced, or even absent. The same also holds true for many who comment on it or pontificate about it, and, astonishingly and disappointingly, for some of those who are charged with developing or applying military strategy. And yet, military strategy is an extraordinarily important subject, if for no other reason than that the United States makes such frequent resort to it. In the interest of greater comprehension of the nature, condition, purpose, and use of this essential instrument of statecraft, it may be instructive to recall some elementary truths about war, identify and explore some of its modern conditions, and, in doing so, to present some general principles and opinionated observations about the present and future of military strategy.

Much that is fundamental about war has changed. What has not changed are the unique, universal, and unavoidable peculiar conditions characteristic of all wars, at all times, in all places, among all enemies: including the immanence of insufficiency, uncertainty, contingency, fallibility, chance, tenuousness, and, of course, the ubiquity of fear, misery, chaos, and pervasive violence; each of these circumstances exacerbates the effects of all others.

🏛 *The nature of strategy*

Classically, military strategy is the employment of violence in a deliberate, rational way for a political purpose. It is imperative and obvious that any military strategy be derived from and be devised to support a national interest, which must be, without exception or equivocation, articulated clearly, precisely, unambiguously, and authoritatively. Deliberate employment presupposes, or at least implies, a well-thought out course of action. Military strategy is founded on the relationship among ends, means, and ways. The ends of military strategy are always political—even when unrecognized or denied. There are no purely military operations conducted for purely military ends. If military operations have no political objective, then they are merely mayhem and murder. No matter how intellectual and artful, brilliantly conceived and elegantly executed, strategy is an exercise of mere meaningless craftsmanship unless it is conducted in pursuit of a political objective. Only when such a political objective is attained is the strategy a success, which is the necessary and exclusive definition of victory.*

Ends are the objectives of a military strategy—and a strategy's resulting resulting operations—sufficient to achieve the specific ends of a policy. Means are the instruments applied to achieve the ends. They consist of the resources of men, money, and *materiel*—including men's exertions, sacrifices, skills, talents, and understanding. Ways are the courses of action, the appropriate

---

* Obviously, the author accepts von Clausewitz's view.

applications of force. However, what means are applied and how the ways are employed, although seemingly leading directly to the ends, may—because of incomplete knowledge, fanatical singlemindedness of pursuit, or failure to appraise and adjust their reception and results—compromise, diminish, undermine, and even overtake or nullify the complete achievement of the desired ends or even become ends in themselves.

The selection of ends, means, and ways must be estimated not only for their obvious and immediate outcomes but also for their indirect and unintended subsequent consequences. Ends, means, and ways must be congruent, continually rebalanced, and synchronized with each other so that they may be mutually supporting; only then are policy and strategy in continuing coherence. Often, however sufficient and synchronized the means and ways to the ends, and however desirable, achievable, realistic, and necessary the ends, the exercise of a persistent, determined will—by policy makers, strategists, and participants, soldiers and civilians—is the singular, critical factor in overcoming the obstacles, sacrifices, and opposition to the achievement of the ends.

Strategy, then, is simply an intellectual attempt to order and direct these factors—ends, ways, and means—and a practical endeavor to apply them to one's own advantage against that of the enemy. Because the causes, courses, and consequences, the purposes and objectives, the means and modes, the costs and risks, and the scope, context, condition, and duration of wars vary widely, there is no single, universal strategy that suits all wars. By definition, each strategy must be unique.

Every strategy is constrained by technology, logistics, training, doctrine, geography, climate or weather, and, in even greater measure, leadership, and also national character.* Above all,

---

* National character is a Victorian conception now out of fashion, yet it has proven to be a necessity in intelligence in twenty–first century warfare. Neither fashion nor political correctness lessen the truth and usefulness of the concept or its analytical and operational relevance. However, how this concept can be applied usefully to multi-cultural nations is problematical.

military strategy is constrained by policy: strategy should derive from, conform to, be directed by, and answer to policy. As such, military strategy is but an instrument, an expression, a means, a mode, and a continuation of policy. Strategy is policy in execution. If strategy is not an arm of policy, it is uncontrolled and worse than directionless; it is a danger to policy and the state itself.

War merits careful consideration because it is the ultimate instrument of statecraft. In some ways, it is a failure of statecraft. Nevertheless, war is a legitimate instrument of statecraft. War is the greatest affair of a people because it risks their very existence: their political organization, their freedom, and their culture. It is so even when undertaken by so-called "non-state entities." Thus, war truly is *ultima ratio*. Because war may threaten existence, before a decision is made to undertake war and to commit to a strategy, leaders must answer: why war is the necessary and ineluctable policy alternative; what kind of war will ensue from both belligerents' actions; what are the enemy's motivations, intentions, expectations, objectives, alternatives, commitments, and capabilities; what will be achieved by war; what costs will both belligerents willingly and unwillingly pay; and what course will end the war should its pursuit bring failure? Beginning with this initial consideration and determination, policy and strategy must be in continuing, absolute, mutual understanding and agreement. This understanding must comprehend the moral, material, physical, psychological, cultural, and circumstantial factors operative in the particular war under consideration.

🏮 *The essentiality of intelligence*

By its very nature, war, in its many parts, is characterized by unknowability and uncontrollability. Since every strategy is based on assumptions, every assumption involves an expectation of a desirable advantage or an admission of inadequate knowledge. Assumptions are among the greatest risks. Hence, all strategy is, by definition, an informed calculation of risk. The replacement of assumptions with facts in turn reduces uncertainty, risk, and, ultimately, costs in blood, treasure, power, influence, credibility, and reputation. However, there are unforeseeable factors that can not be fixed as facts: among them are the "known unknowns" and the "unknown unknowns" that surprise and may disable and compromise any effort when they manifest themselves. Nevertheless, the replacement of assumptions with facts is the task of intelligence. Thus, intelligence is the foundation of strategy. Intelligence is now the predominant principle of warfare: it guides, informs, and permeates the formulation of strategy and the execution of operations.

Intelligence has an indispensable role. Beyond the perennial primary problem of ascertaining elusive intentions and covered capabilities, intelligence is the essential foundation for establishing, delimiting, and understanding both the strategies—one's own and the enemy's—to be applied to the battlespace. In war, the *nonpareil* objective of an attack is the enemy's strategy. Intelligence can best reduce uncertainty by providing an understanding of the enemy's strategy: that is, the enemy's understanding of the battlespace and the enemy's understanding of one's own strategy.

The enemy's strategy can then be shaped and even nullified by deceiving him about one's own strategy and manipulating the development and execution of his strategy, thereby forcing him to conform to one's own strategy and thus setting the terms of the conflict to one's own advantage. Of course, the ability to manipulate an enemy and alter the very framework and factors of a conflict demands timely, extraordinary, and insightful understanding of the enemy—intelligence ideally approximating inside knowledge or intuitive comprehension. The development and execution of a strategy, in any case, has to be founded on an estimate of the enemy's strategy that is based on his calculations, conditions, and constraints that are grounded in the outlook, values, and perceptions of his sometimes radically different structure and culture and approach to warfare. Such an essential understanding of an enemy's strategy, sometimes, is dependent on a penetrating counterintuitive insight into what may be incredible and alien ends, ways, and means that offer startlingly unexpected operational possibilities derived from the enemy's culture and values that are inconceivable in one's own culture and strategy. An acute, penetrating, and insightful understanding of an enemy's outlandish thinking, although extraordinarily difficult, is an essential necessary task of intelligence. Its acceptance is also a necessity for commanders. Of course, it is most difficult to immerse oneself in a foreign and almost unimaginable view of the world, yet it is the obligatory charge of intelligence to understand, to explain, to convince when necessary, and to counter such enemy threats, however exotic they may be. Unfortunately, however necessary, this primary task, is untraditional, not customary, not routine, and therefore too frequently neglected in American intelligence. In the twenty–first century, especially at the strategic level, which includes foreign perceptions of the adequacy of one's power and the ability to exercise it, intelligence must be anticipatory, preclusive, and preemptive even if this risks intelligence exceeding estimation to speculation.

Technology

Today, more than other influences, technology has visibly transformed war, particularly by providing almost absolute and constant awareness of the entire battlespace, truly a paradigm change for intelligence. But intelligence has to provide more than mere information or awareness. After all, awareness is not always understanding. Sensors sense, but do not provide a sure sense of some information. Mere observation of phenomena does not necessarily explain their meaning. Thus, understanding of the battlespace is always incomplete and often incorrect. Intelligence is inherently imperfect; yet, its task is to make the understanding of the battlespace complete, correct, timely, and tailored—in short, relevant, comprehensible, and useful to operations.

In modern times, technology and its tactics have been the essential expression of warfare.

Nevertheless, although technology will not change the essential nature of warfare, it can change the conduct and the outcome of a particular war. Often, technology, because of its awesome attraction, has tended to determine, overwhelm, replace, or exclude strategy. Also, many supposed strategists seem fixated upon a novel technology, having a single-minded reliance on its supposed decisive effect. Notwithstanding this occasional excessive absorption, technology has enhanced, extended, and complicated strategy.

Some specific technologies, in the past, have permanently transformed warfare, and specific technologies continue to transform contemporary warfare. War is now waged in and for the electronic spectrum, and soon war will be waged in, from, and for astronomical space.* The technology that has made war possible in these environments and thereby transformed war by

---

* Should the U.S. go to war against a so-called "peer competitor" state, surely that war will be a space war. Such a war will transform all strategy and warfighting.

creating this new medium of operations is the computer. Indeed, it is the computer that is the engine of the so-called Revolution in Military Affairs, though perhaps not on a par with the invention of gunpowder and nuclear weapons. The dependence of the United States on computers for communications, command and control, intelligence, surveillance, reconnaissance, warning, targeting, weapons control, and battle management systems—in the electronic spectrum and astronomical space—cannot be exaggerated. These systems and all their appurtenances and applications have taken on such essentiality that they themselves have become the subjects and objects of operations. The dependence of modern societies, governments, and military establishments on information and information systems writ large in almost all of their activities—and the increase in information systems and their interdependence worldwide—now offer, simply by their existence, innumerable, incomparable opportunities for hostile exploitation with the possibility of inordinate gains.

⚜ *Cyberwar*

Warfare has always been dependent on information. But today, information dominates warfare, such that wars already are waged essentially with, for, and against information in some form. Some of this is cyberwar—the use of computers to attack information systems controlling parts of an enemy's intelligence, military, policy, political, informational, economic, and social organization, controls, processes, and substance. In military operations, the most consequential value of cyberwar is its inherent unique utility in attacking an enemy's command and control, the mind and nervous system of the enemy leadership. Cyberwar provides the possibility of integrating and complementing actual combat operations with virtual operations, and of substituting some virtual operations for actual operations. Virtual operations can intensify, expand, extend, and augment actual operations. Cyberwar can transform the potentialities of a strategy by imposing on the enemy a false reality in place of an actual reality, causing the virtual to foreclose the veritable. Cyberwar can preempt, misdirect, negate, corrupt, destroy, and, most desirably, control, manipulate, and exploit an enemy's strategy. Cyberwar can subvert the autonomy, integrity, adaptability, and sustainability of an enemy's strategy—and, ultimately, even his policy.

Cyberwar is often considered to be a weapon of mass disruption; it can be a weapon of mass destruction. In either use, the limitations on targets and the control of the intents, effects, collateral damage, and the political and military consequences of cyberwar operations are to date formidable, incomplete, and ethically uncertain, and represent undecided issues of policy, strategy, and intelligence. Equally formidable, incomplete, uncertain, and undecided thus far—and until recently not even considered—are particular uses of cyberwar especially: in deterrence of hostile cyberwar operations alone or of warfare ranging from covert action and guerrilla warfare to conventional and even nuclear, chemical, and or biological operations; in preemption of cyberwar and/or the spectrum of kinetic attacks; and in retaliation with cyber operations in lieu of or combined with kinetic responses or foregoing cyber operations in favor of kinetic responses. In addition to the concerns and characteristics peculiar to cyberwar, its very nature tends toward control and direction at the highest echelon, especially to achieve its most strategic effect. Notwithstanding these concerns and despite cyberwar's latency, its formidable potential is yet to be fully realized. It is doubtful whether national strategic cyber operations encompassing integrated simultaneous political, military, economic, social, intelligence, informational, and psychological measures have the necessary policy, legal, and organizational framework, much less strategies and plans. In fact, the larger issues of the integration of cyberwar capabilities as a military instrument with the other major instruments of national strategy, viz. diplomacy, economic warfare, propaganda, subversion, covert operations, etc. have not as yet been realized. The interdepartmental and interagency integrated employment of cyberwar for the classic missions in pursuit of national interests, namely assurance, deterrence, denial, dissuasion, coercion, compellence, containment, preemption, prevention, and punishment, have not been comprehensively undertaken. Lacking also is the integration of the other instruments of foreign policy with cyberwar in strategic covert and/or clandestine interagency operations short of open combat during ostensible peacetime, including long term preparation of a battlespace against not only a hostile state, its military and intelligence, but also its society, polity, and economy, perhaps as long as several years in advance of the main overt kinetic combat operation.

Deception

The development of cyberwar has raised deception to a new and greater utility in warfare—and in statecraft generally—whose scope, uses, and results in both are yet to be thoroughly explored and exploited. Deception is no longer a mere sometime multiplier or enhancer of force, an occasional operational artifice, or a pro forma adjunct in planning. Deception can be a ubiquitous, constant danger to command, intelligence, counterintelligence, communications—and strategy and policy. Deception uniquely provides the foundation that fabricates an exploitable advantage, distorting fact and deluding with fiction, thereby obscuring the difference between the real and the unreal, and thus destroying rationality in intelligence, strategy, and policy. Because cyberwar operates in the virtual world with actual effects, it is especially suitable to the propagation of deception since deception creates a virtual or false reality. Deception can play a premier role in cyberwar because, by its very nature, cyberwar establishes vulnerabilities and deception is aimed at creating and exploiting vulnerabilities. Deception and cyberwar tend to be mutually reinforcing and to facilitate each other in attacking strategy directly.

The most profitable strategic vulnerabilities exploitable by deception are the intellectual, cultural, and psychological conceptions, assumptions, expectations, and convictions of policy, command, and intelligence on which a strategy is founded—especially the vanities, assumed verities and certainties, mental methodologies, and reflexive reactions—on which a strategy is founded. Attacking these qualities of a leadership can unbalance, disorient, and paralyze an enemy, particularly by delaying the timely accuracy of his situational apprehension, understanding, and reaction. Because the classic so-called principles of war* take on new forms and functions in cyberwar, deception can exceptionally enhance their applications in virtual

* The principles of war are a troublesome misnomer accepted as truthful through age, usage, and authoritative repetition. They are, in practice, principles of operations. Applied to contemporary war and particularly cyberwar, these principles include especially the objective, initiative, unity of effort, mass/economy of force and effort, concentration, maneuver, surprise, and security, and also the universal, ubiquitous contexts of conflicts including friction, fog of war, and centers of gravity. Both the principles and their contexts take on new operational meanings and are not necessarily relevant or applicable in all instances.

operations to produce multitudinous and decisive veritable effects. Deception, therefore, should no longer be regarded as merely a stratagem within a strategy; it now is an independent factor in warfare.

🔯 The meaning of new technologies

Cyberwar is not the only obvious indicator that warfare has been undergoing a fundamental transformation. In fact, a new revolution in military affairs is already underway.* Applying biology, nano-engineering, various kinds of directed energy, remotely operated systems, robotics, and much more to weapons—a new technological asymmetry—poses basic questions about strategic and technological surprise, integration of weapon systems, and the conditions, uses, utility, ethics, and outcomes of war, such as gaining

---

* "The Technology Avalanche" is the term for the vast and increasing amount and pace of technological developments coined by David Evans of the Cisco Corporation.

the initiative, maintaining freedom of action, the limits of operations, and the content of victory. The very conception and understanding of the meaning of operations, and perhaps strategy, may change.

Paradoxically, a near-omniscient situational awareness could constrain strategic thought because of a too fine concern with an enemy's perceptions and responses. Even with a supposedly near-omniscient situational awareness and information dominance, the development of policy, execution of strategy, and conduct of operations may be so constrained by domestic and foreign factors that freedom of political and military action may be problematical and the relationship between force employment and desired political outcome may become tentative and tenuous, and inescapably compromised in conception.

Furthermore, the new weapons and the so-called legacy weapons, as always, will require new organizational forms of integration, concepts of operations, and rules of engagement to exploit their full utility and mutual reinforcement. These adaptations may be the easier of the tasks resulting from the deployment of the new weapons. Maintaining access and presence in geopolitically strategic regions and enforcing influence against hostile states equipped with these new weapons obviously will be much more difficult to achieve than in the presence of legacy weapons alone. Their achievement will be even more difficult against hostile movements and groups to whom the new weapons may be proliferated. The efficacy of military force and its applications may be so constricted that the practical meaning of military superiority, as estimated traditionally, may be rendered irrelevant in particular circumstances. Although the resort to military violence by irregular groups throughout the spectrum of peace and war will continue the overpowering, primary role of military power in forming and controlling the relationships among states and their conduct in the evolving norms of a new international system will be unsettled at best, thus making a break from the past.

Since the end of the Cold War, military operations have changed fundamentally in more elements than cyberwar alone. A remarkable, unexpected, fundamental, and permanent change in warfare is the merging of the traditional three levels of warfare: strategic, operational, and tactical. Weapons and systems associated traditionally with only one of these echelons are employed against objectives and for outcomes at another level—true effects-based operations. Sometimes, the applications have effects at more than one level. The use of tactical forces for strategic results is now common. Similarly, the employment of strategic forces for tactical purposes is also common. It is in the interrelationships of these three levels that decisions beyond traditional employments and expectations may be found. The introduction of the new weapons could provide technological and operational surprise to the achievement of effects and outcomes.

Another and ultimately more consequential development in contemporary warfare is the variable and unstable utility of force. America's enemies cannot now approximate, much less directly oppose, its singular superiority in and its at-will employment of high technology, rapid mobility, high tempo, all-weather, day-night, combined, global precision warfare. Yet, paradoxically, this historically unprecedented, massive military advantage, albeit with so-called legacy weapons, is sometimes inapplicable and irrelevant in contemporary warfare, due to several, diverse, and seemingly unrelated but extraordinarily powerful domestic and foreign constraints.

In recent years, much has been made of asymmetrical warfare—the novel and unorthodox employment of assumedly unsuitable, inadequate, and, of course, unexpected capabilities—as if it were some kind of new warfare, both unheard of and unfair. Asymmetrical warfare is nothing more than an opponent's use of his strengths to best advantage against the identifiable weaknesses of an enemy. It is an astonishingly quaint phenomenon, an unaccustomed arrogance even, that we are still surprised and appalled when native hostiles have the effrontery and impudence not to fight according to our expectations.* It is the contestants, their cause and objectives, their capabilities and weaknesses and consequently their tactics in particular, that by their very nature result in asymmetric and often protracted warfare. Though asymmetric warfare is not necessarily the recourse only of the weaker enemy, it is often the recourse of an enemy who is unencumbered by doctrine, training, and tradition and whose survival is dependent on imagination, invention, and innovation in organization, strategy, operations, and tactics. It is, after all, the application of novel and unorthodox conceptions, such as the imaginative, indirect, unconventional, and therefore un-

---

* A potential consequential change in contemporary war is the different conceptual approach to warfare of Chinese strategists. If and when applied in operations, the Chinese way of war is likely to surprise the U.S. and to upset the equilibrium of U.S. military strategy, notwithstanding the *pro forma* requirement in senior service schools to read a translation of Sun Tzu's treatise.

expected initiatives that can result in surprise, tactical and strategic. Asymmetric warfare is simply an accurate descriptive term; it should not be a pejorative complaint or a defensive excuse. Nor should an enemy's employment of it be discounted because of one's own material plenty, reliance on technology, or recourse to attrition, for this can result in a fatal failure to correct one's own vulnerabilities, be they budgetary, political, technical, intellectual, organizational, psychological, or moral. Many asymmetries can affect the conduct of a war: asymmetries in objectives, capabilities, technologies, resources, tactics, or skills. The most dangerous asymmetry is the inadequacy of conception in policy and strategy.

Insurgency

In contemporary times, for several, varied reasons, insurgency has become a frequent way of warfare, frequently asymmetric in character. Insurgencies have some characteristics in common, yet each insurgency is unique; therefore, counterinsurgencies are not replicable. Historically, insurgencies sought to replace a regime and usurp its power and authority, despite its societal support. They attacked the legitimacy of traditional regimes—the very idea of their right to exist—often by forcing them to fight a war against their own people that sapped their self-confidence and undermined their moral authority. However, the worst, most radical of these classic insurgencies sought to subvert the soul of a society, to obliterate its national character. Some contemporary insurgencies, however, are fundamentally different from historic guerrilla warfare; they are evocative of fantastic notions of the world and its workings and embody all the barbarity, conviction, fanaticism, zealotry, and extravagances of extremists.

The most extreme and potentially the most consequential and dangerous contemporary insurgencies aim to eliminate the very foundations, institutions, traditions, values, principles, beliefs, and allegiances of a political system; indeed, they seek to supplant all states, religions, cultures, societies, and civilizations other than their own. In all, they seek the complete destruction of whatever they oppose. Such unrelenting, ruthless, and radical movements have no possible curbs on their vicious operations and unlimited transcendental aims. Such movements are the starkest examples of a fundamental change in warfare, and indeed in the international system. Such movements are intrinsically and uncompromisingly hostile, not to be dissuaded from death and destruction whilst condemning coexistence in any measure or form, in their struggle to annihilate all existing order and in their ambition to establish a single, exclusive, new international system.

The United States operates against insurgencies with a disabling disadvantage: it seeks stability, often based on accommodation and compromise. As such, the United States is on the defensive. Insurgents disdain and reject accommodation and compromise. This rejection is one of their ultimate strengths, because it preemptively defines the terms of the struggle and the shape of the objective which the opponent must accommodate. Indeed, compromise would deny the insurgents their very purpose. Insurgents require, seek, and create instability. As such, they are on the offensive. The insurgents always have the political, psychological, and, at least initially, operational advantage because the insurgency is fought at their initiative. Moreover, the insurgents routinely employ operational methods and tactics which the United States cannot match without traducing its very foundational principles and values.

The United States has not yet learned how to wage protracted, asymmetric warfare decisively in exotic environments involving seemingly unreasonable demands and irresolvable disputes. In these wars, political and psychological understanding, issues, instruments, expertise, and effects are paramount. Such wars require a nimble and inventive flexibility in policy and operations and, above all, prolonged and impervious resolve, patience, steadfastness, tenacity, and unshakeable and sophisticated political will and commitment—including acceptance of prolonged bloodletting if necessary. Such wars require also a leadership's absolute clarity as to the cause, its costs and consequences, the character of the contestants, and the capability to convince constituents of the necessity for their commitment. Thus far, apparently, this kind of warfare is still inexplicable to American leadership.

Contemporary warfare poses the dreadful potential of a new international system of power relationships—unfavorable to the United States. The American failure to comprehend clearly geopolitical realities and to conduct decisively contemporary war risks a strategic revolution. Thus far, for the long range, the United States has not produced an intellectual conception, institutional organization, and societal comprehension of contemporary warfare to confront its potential menace. The American failure is profoundly affected by elemental factors, mostly peculiarly cultural, including: an unwillingness to commit to protracted intervention; an almost determined ignorance of other peoples; popular detachment from international affairs; our decremented and devolved sovereignty in military interventions; the inconstancy and incoherence of statecraft for the sustainment of superpower status; the inability of Presidents to explain national interests convincingly; the episodic absence of strategic leadership in the executive and legislature; the immediacy and transience of the American political process; the intellectual insularity, political provincialism, and obsolete outlook of the Congress; the insufficient organization of national security institutions and processes; the failure to resort to the integrated strategic use of the several instruments of statecraft; the almost instantaneous—and often incorrect—global notification and explanation of events; the media's unremitting hostility to authority; the elites' behavior destructive of democracy; partisan creation of bogus realities; the abandonment of our history; and the corruption of our national character. These are elemental constraints on the development and application of strategy, indeed of policy. Nevertheless, though these elemental constraints debase and debilitate the conception and application of strategy and policy, they could be mitigated and even eliminated through an extraordinary but improbable effort. However, the absence of—indeed, the denial of the need for and the rejection of—a consensus on Western moral, social, and political values is not amenable to any organizational, legislative, or administrative repair although such values constitute the very foundation of any strategy or policy. Moreover, in a society of self-referential, self-enabling, and self-legitimating citizens, a sustained consensus on a realistic and moral integrated strategy, and indeed policy, may be hardly possible.*

---

* Policies and strategies motivated by leaders' self-delusion or wishful thinking are deliberate rejections of reality, whether they redefine, evade, or simply do not understand reality. Such policies and strategies will fail of this fault alone, thereby imperiling the people for and to whom these leaders are responsible. Regardless of any other motivation, objective, or conduct, for this reason alone—the rejection of reality—such policies and strategies are immoral.

⚔ *The intractability of war*

Some of the universal verities of war have been transformed, though not eradicated, by radical changes in the international system, whose traditional entities, modalities, and values are no longer universally accepted. The aims of wars are no longer exclusively or primarily political. Wars are no longer fought only or even mainly by armies and states; they are now fought by nascent nations, sundry sects, bizarre zealots and obscurantist fanatics who foment extreme movements and or criminal enterprises, and often some complicated combination of these.*

In some contemporary wars, military force has been introduced before other instruments of statecraft have been exhausted or with inadequate coordination with the other instruments, and the relevance and likelihood of success of that use of force have been assumed or overes-

---

* The so-called "traditional principles of war" and Clausewitz's trinity have completely transformed meanings and uses in contemporary war even when they are relevant.

timated. Tragically, some interventions are enjoined without conviction or commitment and even without understanding of the complex problem. Some efforts to contain or solve disputes have resulted in the use of military force prematurely, inappropriately, or unnecessarily, and, of course, ineffectively. In some instances, military force has been applied reluctantly, if not grudgingly, much too late, and niggardly after avoidable costs and worsening of the conflict. In some instances, the kinds of forces, weapons, tactics, and rules of engagement that have been employed have proven unsuitable to the dispute and counterproductive of the objective.

Oftentimes, military force has been introduced without a clear articulation and explication of the national interest involved and a realistic and directing political strategy or, worse yet, in the absence of *any* political strategy. Thus, the military force lacks its essential political context, both for the conduct of military operations and for the subsequent desired political settlement. Without political strategy, military strategy lacks its purpose.* Moreover, in the absence of an adequate political strategy, there may be postulation but no specification of what is success—victory is assumed, not defined. Under such conditions, the political outcomes intended by the use of force are so inadequate in addressing the underlying issues and so incommensurate with the often delusionary expectations of the protagonists that they prove unsatisfactory, inconclusive, and unacceptable. Such applications of force, by definition, are at best a postponement and at worst an avoidable exacerbation of the situation, always with increased risk and cost and decreased possibility of lasting political success. Thus, settlements based on such inadequate political outcomes are unsustainable and impermanent, often merely impelling another more intractable phase of the conflict. Sometimes, the application of military

---

*   In using the term political strategy when applied to contemporary conflicts, the inclusion of appropriate and integrated intelligence, economic, social, informational, psychological, and cyber strategies at a strategic level should be assumed.

force has produced unambiguous tactical but indecisive political results. Moreover, the mere accumulation of operational successes does not result, as is often assumed, in the certainty of a strategic success—operations and outcomes are unrelated. The military success, often superficial to the dispute, is then a strategic irrelevance, and, as such, the military operation is a waste and the political outcome is a failure.

The absence of appropriate political-strategic objectives and an underlying and integrated military-political-economic-informational-intelligence strategy can often result in the sustainment of a process of interminable and indecisive engagement that effectively replaces the striving for a solution and itself is accepted as a success. Process replaces progress; effort substitutes for outcome; confusion and pretense conceal disagreement and indecision; and appearance masquerades as reality. Equivocation, misrepresentation, obfuscation, and vacillation, often deliberate, in imposing decisive settlements are naturally perceived by many within a society as betrayal and abandonment. They can engender a cynical hopelessness, desperation, and sometimes even an explosive rage that express themselves in violent though futile acts against not only the adversary but also the intervening force.

Today, the use of military force, whether massive or measured, seldom yields permanent, worthwhile strategic gains for the price paid, losses suffered, reputation tarnished, and power diminished. In contemporary war there is a disconcerting disconnect between the application of military force and what has traditionally been understood to be a successful political outcome. War is simply no longer definitive. Increasingly, people's expectations of such an outcome are so slim that the willingness to employ military force and the legitimacy of that decision are often in doubt. Similarly, because of this doubt, the effectiveness of the exercise of the other traditional instruments of state power is rendered questionable.*

---

* It is increasingly difficult to apply Scholasticism's just war criteria, especially consistently, to contemporary war, particu-

⚗ *The passing of peace*

No longer do the armed forces alone wage what in fact is war, even though it is seldom termed as such. Sovereignty, independence, and authority are undermined, societies are subverted, cultures are corrupted, and patrimonies are plundered as war is now waged under the cover of many guises and euphemisms for intervention; for example: counterterrorism, sanctions enforcement, resource competition, ethnic autonomy, minorities protection, religious proselytization, nation-building, preemptive defense, and, even, peacekeeping. Most of these are the justifications for external interventions and

---

larly to various insurgencies and cyberwar campaigns. War is not categorically and inherently morally dubious. Who, why, for what, and how a belligerent resorts to war determine whether he meets or fails the criteria. However, there is a seeming difficulty in using the criteria of just war doctrine: They are premised on, relevant to, and descriptive and prescriptive of a traditional warfare that should seldom occur in the twenty first century.

some are also the rationalizations for internal repression. Furthermore, in the age of globalization, financial and commercial arrangements and cyber attacks are marshaled stealthily and ruthlessly to pilfer the wealth, appropriate the intellectual capital, steal the official and proprietary secrets, plagiarize the research, corrupt the political processes, distort the policies, and diminish the power of rival states. Economies are now more open, interdependent, and therefore more vulnerable; as a result, economic warfare measures can be waged more selectively, easily, and surreptitiously—and often legally—when integrated into and covered by normal economic relations. These measures can be targeted strategically to achieve political objectives, to shape the battlespace, and even to subvert the viability and autonomy of a state. Such attacks of varying sophistication, duration, and breadth exemplify the means of contemporary war.

The twentieth century experience with protracted, horrific, extreme violence deliberately employed as systematic terror in external intervention and internal repression has been unprecedented and enormously destructive; more important, it has had profoundly evil, anti-human consequences whose full effects we probably have not yet fully realized. Whether in traditional or contemporary warfare, the twentieth century has left the bloodiest legacy in history. Perhaps the most pernicious part of the legacy is the obliteration of the distinction between soldier and civilian, combatant and non-combatant, the warfront and the home front, and, ultimately, peace and war.

In the past, war was defined as combat between enemies: a temporary resort to violence in a continuing political engagement, after which politics would revert to peaceful means.

There no longer is a significant, practical, and recognizable distinction between war and peace. Peace and war are now fungible in practice. A belligerent may choose one of many open acknowledgements or euphemistic disguises for war, based solely on its apparent expediency and efficacy that best fits his purpose, the manner of conflict and its putative justification. There no longer are periods of war and other than war. There is simply a continuum of war, albeit in different manifestations. If war is politics waged by other means, now politics is war waged by other means. In short, peace is merely war fought at times with armed forms and means and at other times with not necessarily unarmed, non-violent forms and means. Conflict is now a normal and acceptable and almost usual conduct of relations among states.* The very definition of war has changed, but America's leaders have yet to find it in their glossary, and the United States has not recognized the need or learned how to wage constant war as peace.

---

* The thought, ethics, values, and norms of such men as Grotius are considered outmoded and irrelevant. The acceptance of the degraded practices of modern war as norms is one of the pernicious—immoral, really—fundamental and profound subversions of the basis of Western Civilization.

Policy makers evade and muddle identifying and elucidating the abiding fundamental national interests that strategists should pursue—with war when necessary. Indeed, absent too often are the considerations of, much less the answers to, the most basic questions of policy and strategy. So, strategy's foundation is uncertain. Strategy has been confused and conflated with policy. Military strategy, such as it is, is no longer the province solely of generals; its provenance lies more with policy makers—and even more so with politicians. Generals only propose strategies that politicians may impose. Today, military strategy is irreversibly driven by and enmeshed primarily in politics and pretended principle more than in policy. Indeed, all too often, politics serially impels, deforms, and betrays strategy, so much so that, at the highest political and military levels, there is a seriously debilitated ability to understand and formulate strategy. This inability has reached a crisis stage.

Increasingly, strategists have much difficulty in grounding their work on ruthless reality and a penetrating understanding of the enemy, whilst applying clear thinking, intellectual imagination, and a coherent, calculated correlation of capabilities, objectives, exertions, resources, risks, costs, benefits, and outcomes. The autonomy, abstruseness, and distinctiveness of military strategy have been denied by the conditions of modern conflict and policy making. The practice of military strategy as a recondite, expert discipline of a few specialized professionals is an obsolete, antique notion that is no longer tenable. Strategy, then, has become an unceasing, frustrating, and seemingly seldom successful endeavor. Now, military strategy, alone and in itself, is insufficient to a warfare that never again can be confined to the outwitting and killing of an enemy on a battlefield.

The demands of contemporary war, in whatever guise, require for its successful execution much coordination of military strategy with and support from the other instruments of statecraft, including diplomacy, political action, information operations, intelligence, economic warfare, etc. Indeed, strategy should integrate the ends, means, and ways of military force with the ends of national policy and the means and ways of the several other instruments of statecraft. The application of a mutually reinforcing effort against an enemy has to be the result of an integrated orchestration of a planned and sustained national strategy that is suffused with an authentically strategic direction. Unfortunately, in the United States an understanding of this necessity and an organization for its conduct are absent. Neither Congress nor the Executive has a grasp of this need and the political class seems determined to prevent such an understanding. For the enterprise of military strategy, the prospect is unclear and expectation is unwarranted, yet engagement is unavoidable.

All wars are horrible, but, for that, they can be no less useful, effective, necessary, and justifiable. Often they are unavoidable, sometimes indispensable, occasionally preferable, and rarely opportune. War is not a transient aberration. Although wars are usually uncontrollable and seldom are their outcomes fully realized as originally expected; nevertheless, war remains a political act in pursuit of a political objective. As such, war is susceptible to rigorous, rational analysis, and analysis of war is the method of strategy. To understand, to formulate, to apply, to explain, and, above all, to lead a clear, realistic, achievable, and decisive strategy is an essential duty of the decision maker.*

* In the United States, strategic thinking, as opposed to operational thinking, is not sufficiently encouraged among military officers by the Department of Defense, the Services, the Joint Chiefs of Staff, the Joint Commands, and the Service Schools. Too often, strategic thinking is confused with policy, and it is thought to be the province of the civilian leadership.

B rigadier General Walter Jajko, USAF Ret is Professor of Defense Studies at The Institute of World Politics, where he teaches a course in the Theorists of Military Strategy and was the Defense Advanced Research Projects Agency Fellow. He has a degree with honors from the University of Pennsylvania and a graduate degree and certificate from the East European and Russian Institutes of Columbia University and attended post-graduate courses at Harvard University's Kennedy School of Government, the Massachusetts Institute of Technology, and George Washington University's Elliott School of International Affairs. He is a graduate of the Armed Forces Staff College and the Industrial College of the Armed Forces. He served in Southeast Asia. He served in bomber, fighter, reconnaissance, special operations, and intelligence units; as a strategic planner in the Concepts, Strategy, Doctrine Branch, Deputy Chief of Staff, Plans and Operations, HQ USAF; as strategy analyst in the Directorate of Soviet Affairs and as Warsaw Pact analyst in the Estimates Directorate, Assistant Chief of Staff, Intelligence, HQ USAF; as a long range planner in the Office of the Secretary of the Air Force; and as Assistant to the Deputy Chief of Staff, Programs and Resources, HQ USAF. He is a former Director of the Special Advisory Staff, Office of the Secretary of Defense; Assistant to the Secretary of Defense (Intelligence Oversight); Acting Deputy Under Secretary of Defense (Policy Support); and manager of a Presidential program. He retired from the Federal Civil Service as a Senior Executive 6. He has written articles and papers on the Polish RAF fighter squadrons in the Battle of Britain, the Warsaw Rising, intelligence, counterintelligence, command and control, deception, surprise, covert action, psychological operations, information operations, geopolitics, the Balkans, the Kaliningrad Exclave, NATO, Eastern Europe, Poland, Ukraine, and Russia and lectured at the National War College, Joint Military Intelligence College, the Smithsonian Institution, the Hoover Institution, St. Joseph's University, Harvard University's Kennedy School of Government, and Tufts University's Fletcher School of Law and Diplomacy.